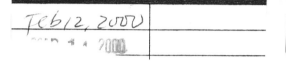
DATE DUE

Feb 12, 2000	
~~4 2000~~	

CRAFTY Puppets

Thomasina Smith

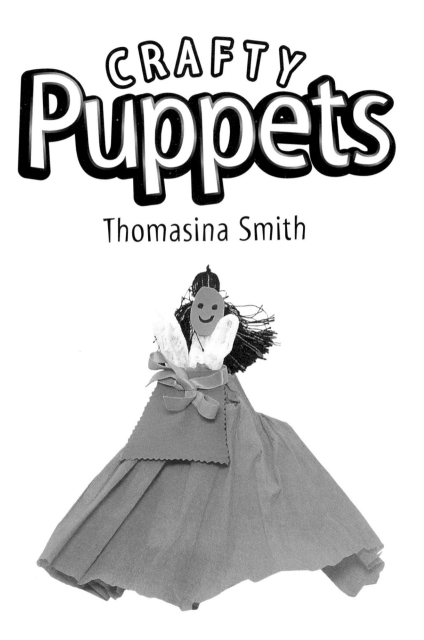

Gareth Stevens Publishing

MILWAUKEE

The original publishers would like to thank the following children for modeling for this book: Kirsty Fraser, Sophia Groome, Nicholas Lie, Tania Murphy, Kim Peterson, Mai-Anh Peterson, Alexandra Richards, Leigh Richards, Alex Simons, Antonino Sipiano, and Maria Tsang. Thanks also to the parents of these children for allowing them to model.

For a free color catalog describing Gareth Stevens' list of high-quality books and multimedia programs, call 1-800-542-2595 (USA) or 1-800-461-9120 (Canada). Gareth Stevens Publishing's Fax: (414) 225-0377.

Library of Congress Cataloging-in-Publication Data

Smith, Thomasina.
    Crafty puppets / by Thomasina Smith.
      p. cm. — (Crafty kids)
    Includes bibliographical references and index.
    Summary: Instructions for making finger puppets, glove puppets, puppets painted on your hands, puppet theaters, and a foot puppet.
    ISBN 0-8368-2480-6 (lib. bdg.)
    1. Puppet making—Juvenile literature. 2. Finger puppets—Juvenile literature. [1. Puppet making. 2. Finger puppets.]
I. Title. II. Series.
TT174.7.S65   1999
745.592'24—dc21
                             99-22878

This North American edition first published in 1999 by
Gareth Stevens Publishing
1555 North RiverCenter Drive, Suite 201
Milwaukee, WI 53212 USA

Original edition © 1996 by Anness Publishing Limited. First published in 1996 by Lorenz Books, an imprint of Anness Publishing Inc., New York, New York. This U.S. edition © 1999 by Gareth Stevens, Inc. Additional end matter © 1999 by Gareth Stevens, Inc.

Assistant editor: Sophie Warne
Photographer: John Freeman
Designer: Michael R. Carter
Gareth Stevens series editor: Dorothy L. Gibbs
Editorial assistant: Diane Laska

Printed in Mexico

1 2 3 4 5 6 7 8 9 03 02 01 00 99

Introduction

Your hands can be bridesmaids, birds, forests, flowers, aliens, and all sorts of other amazing characters. With this book, you can make finger puppets, glove puppets, puppets painted on your hands, and even foot puppets.

You can use your puppets to make up stories with your friends. The fishermen fishing with their net could come across the octopus, or maybe the Tassel family could go to the wedding of the bride with her bridesmaids.

If the idea of making up stories for your puppets captures your imagination, you can make a puppet theater. The two projects for making theaters are very simple. There are also instructions for making props and scenery. Have fun!

Thomasina Smith

Contents

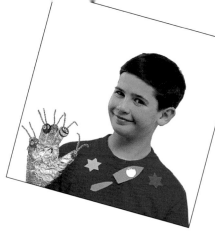

Materials

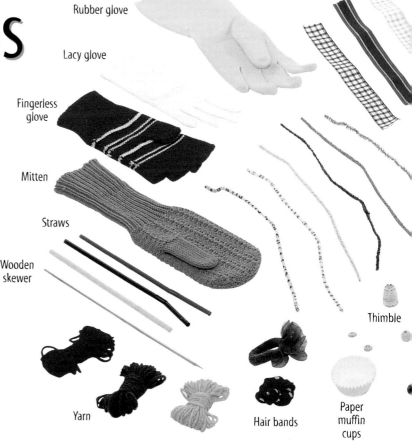

Rubber glove

Lacy glove

Fingerless glove

Mitten

Straws

Wooden skewer

Yarn

Hair bands

Paper muffin cups

Thimble

GLOVES AND SOCKS

Gloves and socks are great for making hand puppets, and mittens make ideal animal puppets. The finger and thumb parts of the mitten make a good nose and mouth. Because gloves and socks come in all sorts of different materials — rubber, lace, wool, nylon — they can be used for many different kinds of puppets.

WOODEN SKEWER

You can find wooden skewers in grocery and hardware stores. They are sometimes sold as barbecue sticks. Ask an adult to trim them with a pair of scissors to remove their sharp ends. You can also use garden sticks, which are made to prop up plants, but they are not as easy to cut.

YARN

Yarn is used to make hair and is good for stitching cut edges. Buy thick yarn and keep any scraps; they might be useful for other projects.

PIPE CLEANERS

You can buy pipe cleaners in craft shops and toy stores. There are many different colors and designs to choose from. Look for brightly colored, striped, and sparkly ones.

THIMBLE

When you are using a needle, always protect your finger with a thimble.

HAIR BANDS

Hair bands come in a variety of sizes, colors, and designs, and they are easy to use because they are elastic and will fit any finger size. They make good puppet hats. You can buy hair bands at any drugstore.

PAPER MUFFIN CUPS

Traditionally used for baking muffins and cupcakes, paper muffin cups come in pastel colors as well as in the standard white.

TULLE

Tulle is an inexpensive fabric. It is easy to use because it doesn't fray when you cut it. It is especially good to use for veils and full skirts.

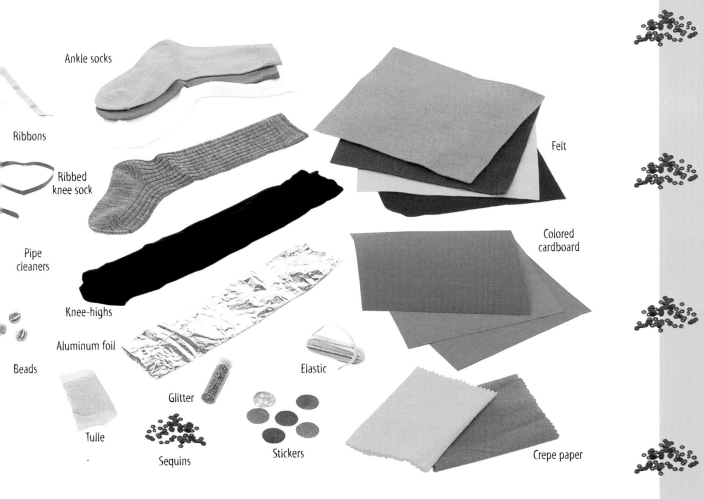

Ankle socks

Ribbons

Ribbed
knee sock

Pipe
cleaners

Knee-highs

Aluminum foil

Beads

Glitter

Tulle

Sequins

Stickers

Elastic

Felt

Colored
cardboard

Crepe paper

GLITTER
Glitter is great for decorating; it adds sparkle to a puppet. Loose glitter, sprinkled on top of glue and left to dry, is best for large areas. Glitter glue sticks are handy for small areas.

ELASTIC
Elastic is available at stores that sell sewing supplies. Look for widths of $\frac{1}{2}$ to 1 inch (1.25 to 2.5 centimeters).

STICKERS
Stickers are perfect for making facial features on puppets. Stationery stores sell them in squares, circles, and rectangles that can be cut into other smaller shapes.

FELT
This pressed fabric is easy to draw on. It does not fray when it is cut, so you do not have to sew the edges.

COLORED CARDBOARD
Use cardboard thin enough to cut easily with a pair of scissors, but thick enough that it will not flop around. When you need to use thicker cardboard, ask an adult to cut it for you with a craft knife.

CREPE PAPER
Crepe paper is like fabric because it bunches up and pleats beautifully.

Equipment

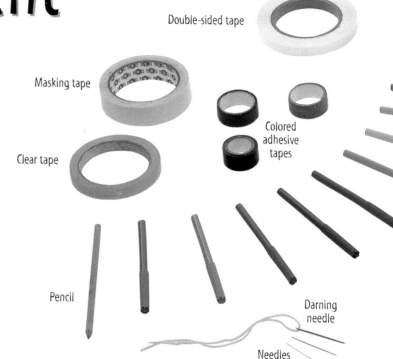

Double-sided tape

Masking tape

Colored adhesive tapes

Clear tape

Pencil

Darning needle

Needles

DOUBLE-SIDED TAPE

Double-sided tape is clear adhesive tape that is sticky on both sides. It is perfect to use on cardboard and fabrics. You simply stick the tape to a surface and peel off the paper backing to uncover the other sticky side. This tape is neat and quick to use.

MASKING TAPE

This paper tape has adhesive on only one side. It tears and peels off surfaces easily, so it is really used only for holding surfaces together while glue is drying. It can then be removed from the surfaces without leaving any marks.

COLORED ADHESIVE TAPES

You can find colored adhesive tapes in electrical and hardware stores. These tapes are good for decoration but do not always have very strong sticking power. Art and stationery stores also have colored tapes, and they are usually a lot stronger.

NEEDLES

When sewing with yarn, use a large embroidery or darning needle. When sewing with thread, use a thin sewing needle. Always wear a thimble to avoid pricking your finger.

MAGIC MARKERS

These markers come in many different colors and have fine, medium, or wide felt tips.

ACRYLIC OR POSTER PAINTS

Both acrylic paints and poster paints are water-based. They are very similar, but poster paints cost less. Although their colors are not quite as strong as acrylic paints, poster paints are good for painting finger puppets and puppet theaters.

WHITE GLUE

Glue comes in many forms. White glue, which might also be called wood glue, comes in plastic containers. You can pour it into a small bowl or use it straight out of the container, and you should apply it with a glue brush. White glue is water-based, so, if you do not need it too thick, you can easily dilute it by adding a little water. Although it takes a long time to dry, when it is dry, white glue is very strong and holds materials together firmly.

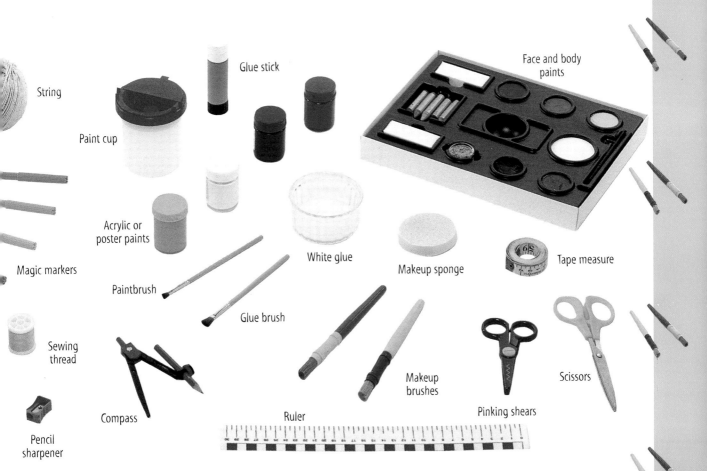

String

Glue stick

Face and body paints

Paint cup

Acrylic or poster paints

White glue

Makeup sponge

Tape measure

Magic markers

Paintbrush

Glue brush

Sewing thread

Compass

Makeup brushes

Scissors

Pencil sharpener

Ruler

Pinking shears

GLUE STICK

A glue stick is the best form of glue to use when sticking a flat sheet of paper onto a flat surface, because the paper will not wrinkle or bubble. Glue sticks dry out quickly, so be sure to replace the top after each use. You can find glue sticks at office and art supply stores.

BASIC ESSENTIALS

A soft pencil and a white eraser are basic essentials of craft equipment. You will need them for every project.

FACE AND BODY PAINTS

You can buy paint specially made for faces and hands. It washes off with water and doesn't irritate skin. Try to buy this paint in a set that includes a makeup sponge, a makeup brush, and makeup crayons, as well as a place to put water. Sometimes the makeup brush supplied in a set can be quite thin, so it is probably worth buying a second makeup brush. You can find one at the cosmetics counter of any drugstore.

SCISSORS

It is best to have two pairs of scissors, one for fabric and one for paper, to keep them from becoming blunt. Pinking shears cut a zigzag edge, so they are very useful for decorating.

RULER

All measurements in this book are given in both inches and centimeters. Some rulers measure only in inches or only in centimeters, and some are marked with both. A tape measure is also a handy piece of equipment.

Basic Techniques

One of the first techniques to master for finger puppets is making a fabric or cardboard tube for each finger. Finger tubes are the basis for these puppet characters.

FINGER TUBES

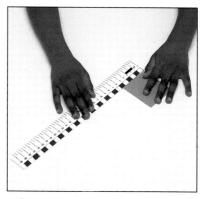

1 Cut a piece of cardboard 3 inches (7.5 cm) wide and about 1 inch (2.5 cm) longer than your middle finger. Wrap the cardboard around your middle finger and trim the end.

2 Measure the height of this piece of cardboard.

3 Draw five rectangles the same size as this piece of cardboard.

10

  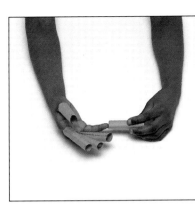

④ Cut out the rectangles.

⑤ Stick a piece of double-sided tape along one side edge of each cardboard rectangle. Wrap a rectangle around each finger and seal it along the taped edge. Each finger will be slightly different.

⑥ Put the puppet tubes onto your fingers and decorate them.

SEWING OR GLUING ONTO A SOCK OR MITTEN

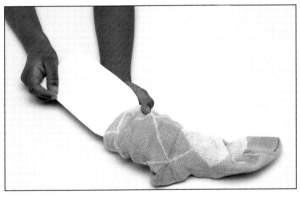 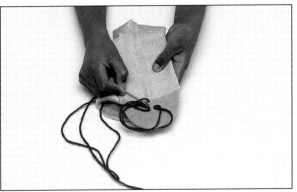

① When decorating a sock or mitten, first draw the shape of the sock or mitten on a piece of thin cardboard and cut it out. Make the shape slightly wider than the sock or mitten. Then insert the cardboard into the sock or mitten to stretch it.

② The cardboard will flatten the sock or mitten so it is easier to decorate. It also prevents you from sewing or gluing through to the other side!

Hand Painting

When you apply paint to your hands, use special face and body paints so they will not irritate your skin. Always let the paint dry thoroughly before applying a different color — otherwise, your masterpiece will become a mess!

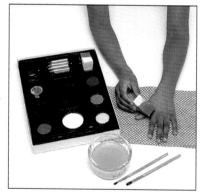

1 Lay out a disposable cloth to protect your work surface. Dip a makeup sponge in water and move it around in the paint to build up a good amount on the sponge. Paint your hand with the sponge.

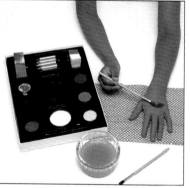

2 Let the paint dry for a minute or two, then apply another layer and let it dry completely. Use a brush to paint on details. Let each color dry before you start using another color.

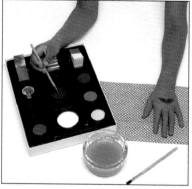

3 You should have separate bowls of water in which to clean each different paint color from your brushes and sponges. Change the water after it has been used a lot.

Painting Features

By holding your hands in different positions, you can make lots of shapes and all kinds of characters, including a stag, a wolf, an octopus, and a soccer player.

1 First, apply base paint to your hand, as described on page 12. To make a mouth, pinch your thumb to the tips of your fingers.

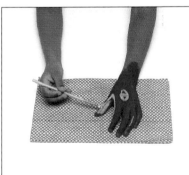

2 Paint your hand in a clenched position first. Then relax the hand and spread it out while you add more details.

Tassel Family

This family of finger puppets has incredibly colorful hair made from tassels. The Tassel family's mother is on one hand and her children are on the other. You can find tassels at a fabric store that sells craft and sewing supplies.

YOU WILL NEED
- Pair of lace gloves
- Needle
- Thread
- Five medium tassels and one large tassel
- Scissors
- Crepe paper
- Ruler
- Pinking shears
- Pink and blue cardboard
- Double-sided tape
- Magic marker
- Thin ribbon

1 Place the gloves in front of you with the palms up. On one glove, stitch the large tassel to the back of the middle finger to make the mother's hair. Sew the five smaller tassels to the fingertips of the other glove to make the children's hair.

2 Cut a rectangle of crepe paper, 3 inches (7.5 cm) by 8 inches (20 cm). Gather up one long side until it is about 4 inches (10 cm) long. Use the pinking shears to cut an apron out of blue cardboard. Tape the apron to the middle of the crepe paper. Stick another piece of tape on the back of the crepe paper along the gathered edge, but do not peel the backing off the tape yet.

3 Draw and cut six small circles out of pink cardboard to make the puppets' faces. Draw features on the faces with a magic marker. Stick the faces onto the fingertips of the gloves using small pieces of double-sided tape.

4 Now peel the backing off the double-sided tape along the gathered edge of the crepe paper skirt. Place the skirt, sticky side up, on your work surface. Press the mother puppet's glove onto the tape and wrap the skirt around the three middle fingers of the glove. Be sure to leave enough room for your fingers to fit inside! Tie thin ribbon around the mother's waist, and the Tassel family is ready for some fun.

Sweater Gang

A fingerless glove is great for making a group of finger puppets wearing sweaters. Simply wear another glove made of lace or a thin fabric under the fingerless glove. The fingertips of the inside glove will be the faces of your puppets. You can design a different outfit for each finger.

YOU WILL NEED

- Fingerless glove
- Small buttons
- Needle
- Thread
- Scissors
- Felt
- Ribbon
- Colored cardboard
- Magic markers
- Thin glove (lace or nylon)
- White glue and glue brush
- Hair bands

1 Put your hand partway into the fingerless glove and carefully sew small buttons down the inside of one of the fingers. Cut a necktie shape out of a scrap of felt and sew it onto another finger. Then, sew a ribbon bow tie onto a third finger.

2 Cut circles for faces out of the colored cardboard and draw features on the faces with the magic markers.

3 Put on the thin glove and pull the fingerless glove on over it. Then pull both gloves off together so the thin glove stays inside the fingerless one. Glue the cardboard faces onto the fingertips of the inner glove.

4 Decorate a couple of the fingers with hats made from hair bands.

17

Aliens

If you enjoy science fiction, why not make some alien finger puppets? These aliens have bodies made of aluminum foil that fits tightly over your hand. Their faces are made from large and small paper stickers in very bright colors, and they have long antennae to pick up radar signals.

YOU WILL NEED
- Scissors
- Aluminum foil
- Clear tape
- Tinsel pipe cleaners
- Ruler
- Stickers
- Magic marker

1 Cut out five rectangles of aluminum foil, just larger than your fingers, and wrap one around each finger. Fasten the foil with plenty of clear tape to make it strong so it does not rip. Now cut a piece of foil big enough to cover your hand. Remember that you will need less foil on the thumb side of your hand.

2 Wrap the foil around your hand and cover it with clear tape. You will probably need several layers of tape to completely seal all of the cracks.

3 Cut several pipe cleaners into pieces about 2 inches (5 cm) long. Carefully attach two pieces of pipe cleaner to each fingertip with clear tape.

4 To make the aliens' faces, attach large, colorful stickers to your foil fingertips. Hologram stickers are perfect. Add small dot stickers to the faces for eyes and use magic marker to draw spots on the dots for pupils. Cut some stickers into mouth shapes and add them to the faces.

Flower Fingers

This flower garden is very easy to make, and it is bright and colorful, too. Paper muffin cups make great petals — buy colored ones or paint some white ones yourself.

YOU WILL NEED

- Scissors
- Colored cardboard
- Ruler
- Pencil
- Double-sided tape
- Paper muffin cups
- Acrylic paints
- Paintbrushes
- White glue and glue brush

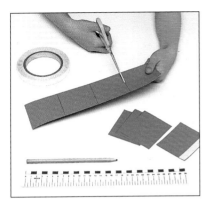

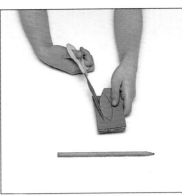

1 Cut a piece of green cardboard and form a tube to fit around your middle finger. Measure this piece of cardboard, then draw and cut out 10 more pieces the same size. Stick a piece of double-sided tape along the side edge of each cardboard rectangle.

2 Peel the backing off the double-sided tape. Then roll the tubes to fit around each finger before sticking the edges together.

3 Fold a piece of green cardboard into several layers. Draw a leaf shape on the top layer and cut it out. This is a quick way to make leaves that are the same size. You will need to repeat this step three or four times to make at least 10 leaves for your flowers.

4 If you are using white muffin cups, paint them different colors. Then cut out circles of colored cardboard and glue them in the bottoms of the muffin cups to make the centers of the flowers. Paint little dots of color on the center of each flower.

5 Glue the muffin cup flowers and the cardboard leaves onto the tube stems with white glue. Let the glue dry completely before putting the flowers on your fingers.

Winter King and Queen

This royal family lives in a winter wonderland. The king, queen, and prince finger puppets are all dressed in white cloaks made from fake fur.

HANDY HINT

It is easier to cut fake fur on the back side of the fabric than the front, especially if you need to cut an accurate shape or size. Draw your shape on the back of the fur before you start cutting.

YOU WILL NEED

- Fake fur
- Ruler
- Scissors
- Colored cardboard
- Double-sided tape
- Magic markers
- Star stickers

1 Cut a piece of fake fur, 8 inches (20 cm) by 4 inches (10 cm), and fold this rectangle in half to make a square. Cut three holes in the folded edge. Make the holes big enough to push your three middle fingers through them.

2 Cut three rectangles out of cardboard for the puppets' faces and three crowns of different shapes and colors. Each rectangle should be wide enough to wrap around a finger with a ½ inch (1.3 cm) overlap. Tape a crown to the top of each face. Draw in facial features with magic markers.

3 Wrap the puppets' heads around each finger and stick the back seam together firmly with double-sided tape.

4 Also, stick the sides of the fur cloak together with double-sided tape.

5 Decorate each crown with a star sticker. Then put the fur glove onto your hand and the three finger puppets onto your fingers.

Angels

A host of angels is especially appropriate to make at Christmastime. This heavenly pair looks very festive with their tinsel wings and their robes edged in gold ribbon.

YOU WILL NEED
- White felt
- Ruler
- Scissors
- Gold ribbon
- Double-sided tape
- Colored cardboard
- White glue and glue brush
- Magic markers
- Sparkly pipe cleaners

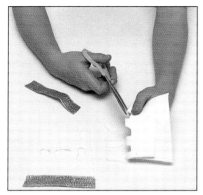

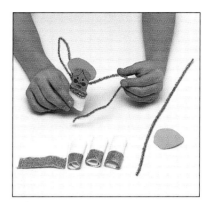

1 For each of the angels' dresses, cut a rectangle, 4 inches (10 cm) by 5 inches (12.5 cm), out of white felt. Fold over 2 inches (5 cm) of the rectangle along its length and cut three finger holes into the fold. Trim each piece of felt into a dress shape. Decorate each dress by attaching gold ribbon to the bottom edge with double-sided tape.

2 Cut two rectangles, 2 inches (5 cm) by 3 inches (7.5 cm), out of pink cardboard and two rectangles, 1 inch (2.5 cm) by 3 inches (7.5 cm), out of white felt. Edge each piece of felt with gold ribbon, glue it onto a pink rectangle, roll it into a tube, and tape the seam closed. Curve the tops of the pink heads and draw on faces and hair.

3 Finish the angels by taping on round halos cut out of yellow cardboard. Twist sparkly pipe cleaners into wing shapes and tape them to the backs of the angels' necks. Cut four rectangles, ½ inch (1.3 cm) by 3 inches (7.5 cm), out of white felt, edge each one with a strip of ribbon, roll it into a tube, and tape the back seam closed.

4 To assemble your finger puppet angels, put your hand through the finger holes of the felt dress. Then put the sleeves on your first and third fingers and the head on your middle finger. You will need help putting on the second angel.

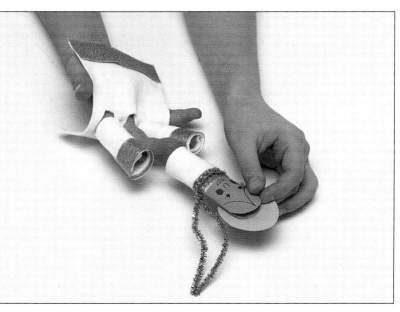

Bride and Bridesmaids

You can have great fun giving this bride's bridesmaids different facial expressions. Here, one is in a very bad mood! Use tulle to make the bride's veil and the bridesmaids' skirts. Why not also make a groom and a best man for the other hand?

YOU WILL NEED
- Ruler
- Pencil
- Scissors
- Colored cardboard
- Felt
- White glue and glue brush
- Magic markers
- Double-sided tape
- Paper
- Tulle (in different colors)
- Ribbon

1 For the bridesmaids' faces, cut four rectangles, 1½ inches (3.8 cm) by 3 inches (7.5 cm), out of colored cardboard. Then cut four pieces of colored felt, 1 inch (2.5 cm) by 3 inches (7.5 cm). Glue a piece of felt over the bottom half of each piece of cardboard. Draw features and hair on the bridesmaids' faces with magic markers.

2 Fit a bridesmaid puppet around each of your first, third, and fourth fingers, as well as around your thumb. Hold the back seams together with double-sided tape.

4 Cut a 3-inch (3.8-cm) square of tulle for a veil. Gather it into a bunch and bind the bunch with clear tape. Then attach a paper bow. To make a skirt, cut a piece of tulle 6 inches (15 cm) by 8 inches (20 cm). Cut two 20-inch (50-cm) pieces of ribbon and stick double-sided tape along one piece. Gather the skirt and stick it to the middle of the ribbon. Stick the other ribbon over the top.

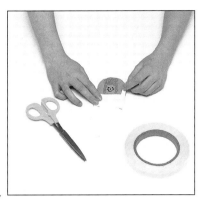

3 To make the bride's face, cut a rectangle, 1½ inches (3.8 cm) by 3 inches (7.5 cm), out of pink cardboard. Cut the top edge into a curve. Draw on features and hair with magic markers. For the bride's dress, cut a piece of white felt, 3 inches (7.5 cm) by 8 inches (20 cm). Glue the dress to the face ½ inch (1.3 cm) from the edge.

5 Tie the ribbon around your hand to attach the skirt. Then put the bridesmaids on your fingers and thumb and the bride on your middle finger. Don't forget her veil!

Fishermen and Fishing Net

This colorful group of puppet fishermen has waterproof raincoats and hoods. They have caught a lot of fish — including one that looks suspiciously like a shark. Will they be strong enough to haul in all those fish? Fishnet stockings make a great net, and bright yellow rubber gloves are perfect for the raincoats and hoods.

YOU WILL NEED

- White and colored cardboard
- Pencil
- Scissors
- Dot stickers
- Magic markers
- Fishnet stocking
- Adhesive tape
- Pair of yellow rubber gloves
- Glue stick

1 Make at least six fish by folding a piece of orange cardboard into several layers, drawing a fish on the top layer, and cutting it out. Also draw and cut out a cardboard shark.

2 Decorate the fish with dot stickers for eyes. Draw in the eyes and teeth of the shark with a black magic marker.

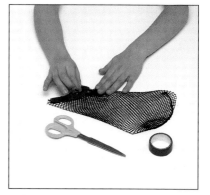

3 Draw the shape of a net on white cardboard and cut it out. Insert the cardboard into a fishnet stocking. Cut off the stocking at the top of the cardboard and tape down the cut edge.

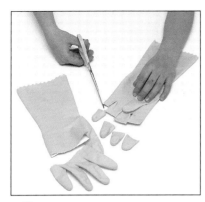

4 Cut the four fingers off of one rubber glove so the fingers are still all joined at the bottom. Then cut four fingertips off the other rubber glove.

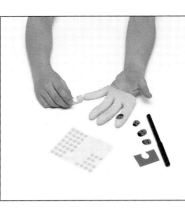

5 Cut four circles out of colored cardboard and draw a bearded fisherman's face on each one. Cut a small hole in one side of each rubber fingertip to make a hood. Put on the glove fingers and top each finger with a hood. Glue on the faces so they look as if they are peeking out of the hoods. Add dot stickers down the fronts of the raincoats for buttons. Glue the fish onto the net and tape the net along the bottom edge of the glove.

Animals in the Forest

On one hand, your fingers are a forest; on the other hand are all the forest animals. When you put your hands together, you can see a fox, a wolf, a tiger, and a badger peeking through the trees!

YOU WILL NEED
- Ruler
- Pencil
- Scissors
- Colored cardboard
- Acrylic paints
- Paintbrush
- Double-sided tape
- Cotton
- Glue stick
- White glue and glue brush
- Disposable cloth
- Face paints
- Makeup brush

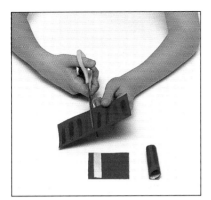

1 Cut four 2-inch (5-cm) by 3-inch (7.5-cm) rectangles out of cardboard for tree trunks. Paint on stripes to look like bark. Stick a piece of double-sided tape down one short edge of each rectangle. Wrap these pieces of cardboard around your fingers and seal their back seams together to make tubes.

2 Cut four treetop shapes out of colored cardboard. Use a glue stick to attach a wad of cotton to each treetop. Paint the cotton with green acrylic paint and let the treetops dry.

3 Glue the treetops to the tree trunk tubes with white glue and let the glue dry.

HANDY HINT

Cotton makes really great fluffy trees. You can buy several kinds of cotton at most drugstores, but the most useful kind comes in a roll.

4 Rest the back of your hand on the cloth and paint animals on your fingers with face paints and a makeup brush. Remember to clean the brush before changing paint colors, and let each color dry on your skin before you apply the next one.

Octopus

With the help of face and body paints, you can make your fingers look like the tentacles of an octopus. Paint circles to look like the suction pads on the underside of the octopus.

YOU WILL NEED
- Disposable cloth
- Face paints
- Makeup sponge
- Makeup brush

HANDY HINT
Always clean your makeup sponge and brush between colors; otherwise, the paint colors will mix together. Also, if you use a towel instead of a disposable cloth, make sure it is an old towel so it will not matter if it gets stained.

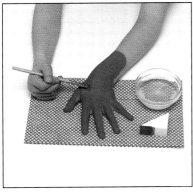

1 Rest your hand on the cloth and apply a coat of blue face paint to your hand and wrist with a makeup sponge. Let the paint dry for a few minutes, then add another coat with a makeup brush. Let the paint dry thoroughly.

2 Turn your hand over and paint your palm pink. To make a good pink color, mix red and white face paints on a makeup sponge, then apply the paint to your skin. Apply a second coat of pink paint with a makeup brush.

3 With your palm up, paint white spots down each of your fingers with the makeup brush. Let the spots dry for a few minutes, then paint around each one with a fine line of black face paint. Let the paints dry thoroughly.

4 Turn your hand over and paint the face of the octopus onto its blue head.

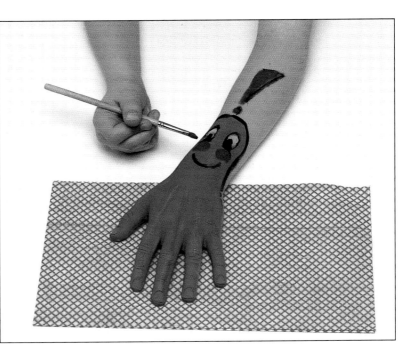

Painted Stag

This painted hand puppet captures the elegance of a proud stag. The shape of the stag is formed by using the first finger and the little finger as horns and the two middle fingers and the thumb as a nose and mouth. The stag's magnificent antlers and large eye are made out of colored cardboard.

YOU WILL NEED

- Disposable cloth
- Face paints
- Makeup sponge
- Makeup brush
- Pencil
- Scissors
- Colored cardboard
- Masking tape
- Glue stick

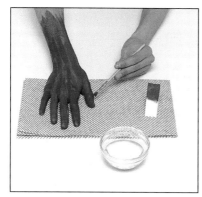

1 Rest your hand on the cloth and apply a coat of brown face paint to your hand and wrist with a makeup sponge. Let the paint dry, then add a coat of lighter brown paint using a makeup brush.

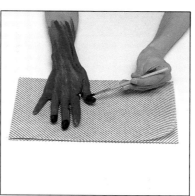

2 Use a makeup brush to paint the tips of your thumb and two middle fingers black.

3 Pinch your fingers and thumb together to make a stag shape. Outline the stag's eye, with white paint, in the oval formed by your fingers. Paint a black line around the eye outline. Then add eyelashes.

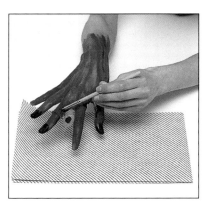

④ To finish the stag's eye, cut a circle out of blue cardboard and paint a black dot in the middle of it. Next, draw antlers on colored cardboard and cut them out, leaving tabs at the base that are long enough to wrap around your finger. Attach the stag's eye to your middle finger with masking tape.

⑤ Paint over the masking tape that is holding the stag's eye in place so it blends in with the paint on your finger. Wrap the tabs at the bottom of each antler around your finger and glue the tabs together. Wear one antler on your little finger and one on your first finger.

Soccer Player

This puppet is a favorite with sports fans. Use your fingers as legs, and see if you can score a goal with the ball. Try to think of other ways to use your fingers as legs, then experiment with more hand painting. Maybe you could make a dancer!

YOU WILL NEED
- Disposable cloth
- Face paints
- Makeup sponge
- Makeup brush
- Ping-Pong ball
- Acrylic paints
- Paintbrush

1 Rest your hand on the cloth and apply a coat of white face paint to one hand with the makeup sponge. Let the paint dry thoroughly.

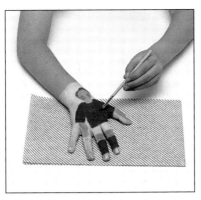

2 Use the makeup brush to paint on red socks and a red shirt. Then paint a face, arms, and knees with pink face paint. Make pink paint by mixing red and white.

3 When the pink paint is dry, outline your soccer player with black paint. Then paint black boots and the features of his face.

4 Paint a Ping-Pong ball with black acrylic paint. When the black paint is dry, carefully paint white markings on your soccer ball. World Cup finger puppet soccer, here we come!

Waltzing Couple

Transform your socks into a dancing couple. You can dress the woman in a beautiful boa and the man in a top hat and bow tie.

YOU WILL NEED

- Two socks (in different colors)
- Scissors
- Ruler
- Felt
- Colored cardboard
- Double-sided tape
- Red colored pencil
- Scrap paper
- White glue and glue brush
- Magic markers
- Ribbon
- Needle
- Thread
- Feather trim

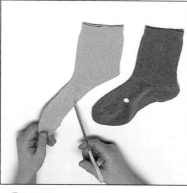

1 Fold each sock lengthwise and cut a small hole through each one, about halfway between the toe and the heel, to make holes on both sides of each sock. The holes should be big enough for your thumb to fit through.

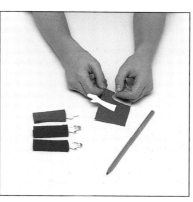

2 Cut four pieces of felt, each approximately 2 inches (5 cm) by 3 inches (7.5 cm). Draw four arms, with hands, on cardboard and cut them out. Tape one arm to the center of each piece of felt and attach a strip of double-sided tape along one edge. Draw fingernails on the hands with the red pencil, then wrap each sleeve around the finger you will wear it on and press along the back seam to tape it closed.

3 To make the woman's hair, draw around your three middle fingers on a piece of scrap paper. Make the bottom edge straight, but draw a curve around the top, about ½ inch (1.3 cm) from the ends of your fingers. Cut out this shape and use it as a template to cut two pieces of felt. Cut a semicircle out of the bottom of one of the felt shapes. Glue the shapes together along three sides to form a pouch.

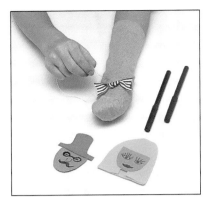

4 Cut two faces out of colored cardboard and draw features on them with magic markers. Glue or tape the woman's face onto her hair and decorate the man's face with a cardboard hat. Make a bow tie for the man from an 8-inch (20-cm) length of ribbon. Sew it onto one of the socks just above the holes. Then glue or tape the man's face onto the sock above the bow tie.

5 Put your hand into the other sock and pull the woman's head over the top of it. Push your fingers through the holes in the sides of the sock and put the woman's sleeves over your fingers. Finish the woman by draping about 20 inches (50 cm) of feather trim around the sock for the boa. Put your free hand into the man's sock and put his sleeves over your fingers.

Big Beaky Bird

This puppet is very simple to make, yet it is amazingly expressive. You move its beak by putting your thumb in the lower part and your fingers in the upper part. With a little practice, you will be able to pick things up with the beak. By moving your arm and wrist, you can make the bird look shy, sleepy, hungry, happy, or just plain mad!

YOU WILL NEED
- Compass
- Ruler
- Pencil
- Colored cardboard
- Scissors
- Double-sided tape
- White glue and glue brush
- Yellow and orange crepe paper
- Black tape
- Black knee-high

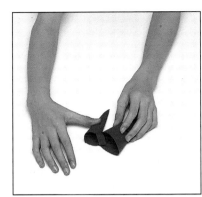

1 Make two cones for the bird's upper and lower beaks. Using a compass, a ruler, and a pencil, draw two semicircles on orange cardboard; one with a 6-inch (15-cm) radius, the other with a 4-inch (10-cm) radius. Cut out the semicircles, leaving a 1-inch (2.5-cm) by 1½-inch (3.8-cm) tab on the smaller one.

2 Roll each semicircle into a cone and stick the edges together with double-sided tape. Stick the tab on the smaller cone inside the larger cone to hold the upper and lower beaks together.

3 To make the bird's plume, fold yellow crepe paper into a fan shape and glue the folds together. Then glue a few strips of orange crepe paper onto the front of the fan shape.

4 Cut two ovals out of white cardboard and two smaller circles out of blue cardboard. Glue the circles to the ovals to make the bird's eyes. Glue the eyes and the plume inside the top part of the beak. Cut pieces of black tape to make pupils for the eyes and nostrils for the beak.

5 Cut a hole in the black knee-high, large enough for your thumb to fit through. Put the knee-high over your hand and arm. Then place your thumb in the bottom of the beak and your fingers in the top.

Goofy Horse

One of the simplest ways to make a glove puppet is to use a mitten. The teeth and eyes on this horse puppet make it look very silly.

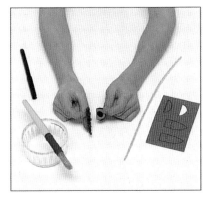

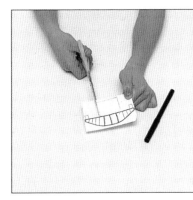

1. To make a mane for the horse, thread the darning needle with yarn and sew a tight stitch at the end of the mitten. Leave a loop approximately 2 inches (5 cm) long, then make another tight stitch in the mitten. Repeat this step all the way up the mitten. Finish by knotting the yarn. Cut through the end of each loop to make a shaggy mane.

2. Draw ears and eyes on colored paper and cut them out. Each eye has a colored eyelid, a blue circle for the eyeball, and ½-inch (1.3-cm) pieces of pipe cleaner, glued on with white glue, for eyelashes. Allow plenty of time for the glue to dry.

3. Draw a row of teeth, about 2 inches (5 cm) long, on a piece of white cardboard with a magic marker. Draw three tabs, two small and one large, along the top of the row of teeth. Cut out the teeth and the tabs.

4. Form the teeth into a curve by attaching the two small tabs to the large one with double-sided tape.

5. Put the mitten on your hand. Glue or tape the eyes, ears, and teeth onto the mitten and let the glue dry completely. Finally, attach reins made from pipe cleaners.

43

Mermaid

This fancy puppet is made from a sock. She is a glamorous mermaid, so her tail and bikini top are decorated with shimmering sequins. You could also glue on metal buttons, bits of foil, or other shiny materials to make your mermaid sparkle even more! Her lustrous hair and the features of her face are made with colored yarn.

YOU WILL NEED
- Scissors
- Cardboard
- Sock
- Yarn (in different colors)
- Darning needle
- Ruler
- Pencil
- Colored cardboard
- Tulle
- White glue and glue brush
- Sequins

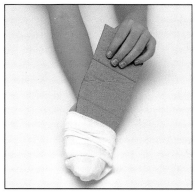

1 Cut out a long cardboard rectangle with a curve at one end. Push the cardboard inside the sock to keep the sides of the sock apart while you sew.

2 Use a darning needle and yellow yarn to sew 3-inch (7.5-cm) loops along the top of the sock for the mermaid's hair. After each loop, make a stitch in the sock to hold the loop in place. Sew the outline and features of the mermaid's face using different colors of yarn.

3 Draw the mermaid's tail on blue cardboard and cut it out. Cut a piece of tulle in the shape of the tail and glue it onto the cardboard, slightly crumpled. Cut a bikini top out of red cardboard. Use white glue to attach sequins to the front of the tail and the bikini top.

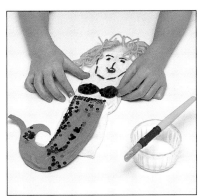

If you do not have any sequins,
you can use glitter instead — your
mermaid will shimmer just as brightly!

4 Glue the mermaid's tail onto
the sock at your wrist and glue
the bikini top just above the tail. Let
the glue dry completely. For a
finishing touch, cut through some of
the loops of yarn in the mermaid's
hair so it will hang down.

Sock Serpent

This bright red snake puppet is made from a pair of tights, so it covers your whole arm when you wear it. The snake has an enormous forked tongue. Did you know that snakes use their tongues instead of their noses to smell?

YOU WILL NEED
- Scissors
- Pair of tights
- Pencil
- Thin cardboard
- Double-sided tape
- Magic marker
- Yarn
- Darning needle
- Felt
- White glue and glue brush
- Beads

① Cut one leg off of the pair of tights. It should be long enough to cover your whole arm. Cut the foot off of the other leg, just below the heel. Draw around the foot on thin cardboard and cut the foot shape out.

② Turn the foot piece inside out. Fold over the cut edges and stick them down with double-sided tape. Then turn the foot piece so the right side is out again and push the cardboard shape inside to stiffen it. This foot piece will be the lower part of the snake's mouth.

③ Pull the snake's body over your arm and make a mark where your thumb is. Then remove the snake and cut a small hole for your thumb. You will use your thumb to move the lower half of the snake's mouth when it is in place. Thread a darning needle with yarn to sew the top edge of the foot piece to the snake's body, just above the thumb hole.

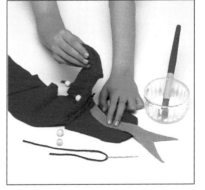

④ Cut a forked tongue out of felt and glue it inside the snake's mouth. Then sew a bead on each side at the top of the snake's head to make its eyes. Finally, cut two small semicircles out of felt and glue them above the snake's eyes to make its eyebrows.

Elephant

This puppet is made from a pair of gray socks. Your fingers will form the back of the elephant's head and your thumb will be the elephant's mouth. When you move your thumb up and down to open and close its mouth, the elephant's trunk will move up and down, too.

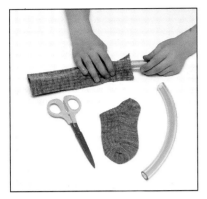

① Cut across one sock, just above the heel. The long part of the sock will be the elephant's trunk. Cut a piece of plastic tubing the same length and place it inside the long part of the sock.

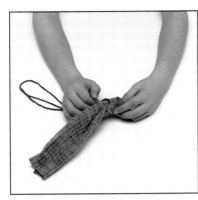

② Pull the sock tightly around the tube. Then thread a darning needle with yarn and sew the sock together, halfway along its length, to hold the tube firmly in place.

③ With the needle and thread, sew buttons on the foot of the other sock to make the elephant's eyes. Cut a small hole in the heel, large enough for your thumb to fit through. Sew the trunk opening to the sock with yarn just above the hole.

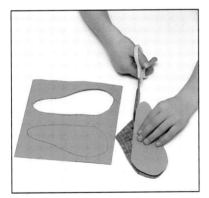

④ To make the elephant's ears, cut the foot left over from the first sock into two pieces. Draw two ear shapes on colored cardboard, using the pieces of sock as guides, and cut them out. Stick a piece of sock onto each cardboard ear shape with double-sided tape and trim the sock piece to fit the cardboard.

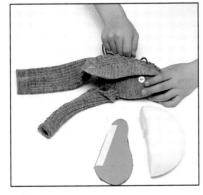

⑤ Cut the bath sponge in half and stuff one half into the elephant's head to pad its face. Then, attach the ears. First, use double-sided tape to hold the ears in place. Then with the darning needle and yarn, sew the ears to the elephant's head to hold them on more securely.

49

Happy Woman, Blue Man

A fun variation on the hand puppet is a foot puppet. Socks have never been so weird! Here, each foot represents a different mood, with a happy, smiling woman in pink and a sad-faced man in blue. These puppets are lots of fun, so why not make some for your friends, too?

YOU WILL NEED
- Scissors
- Cardboard
- Two socks (in different colors)
- Felt
- Glue stick
- Needle
- Thread
- Ribbon
- Beads or buttons

1 Cut out two pieces of cardboard and slide one piece inside each sock. The cardboard must be slightly larger than the sock, so it will stretch the sock.

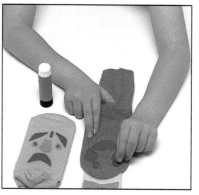

2 Cut cheeks, lips, nose, eyes, eyebrows, hair, and a bow out of the felt. Give each sock a different expression. Glue the felt features onto the bottom of each sock.

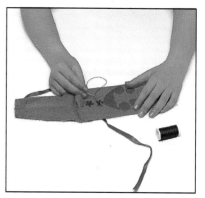

3 Sew the middle of a piece of ribbon to the happy woman sock from the inside of the sock. Then sew on beads or buttons for extra decoration.

4 Tie the ribbon on the happy
woman sock into a bow. Then
remove the cardboard insert from
each sock and put the puppets on
your feet.

51

Peacock Glove Puppet

Peacocks fan out their beautiful feathers to impress peahens. With this glove puppet, you can open and close your fingers to mimic the movements of a peacock.

YOU WILL NEED

- Ruler
- Thin glove
- Colored cardboard
- Magic marker
- Scissors
- Felt
- White glue and glue brush
- Sequins

1 Measure the length of the glove's middle finger and add 1 inch (2.5 cm). Fold a piece of colored cardboard into several layers and draw a feather shape to that measurement on the top layer. Cut out the feathers. Make a total of five.

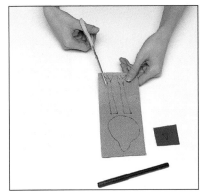

2 Now measure the glove from the wrist opening to the base of the fingers. Draw the body and legs of the peacock on felt to that measurement. Draw a beak on a small piece of pink or red felt and cut it out. Stick the bird's legs to its body and its beak to its face.

3 Draw in the main shaft and other details of the peacock's feathers with the magic marker. Then gently dab some sequins with white glue and stick the sequins onto the feathers. Glue two more sequins onto the bird's face to make its eyes.

4 Glue the feathers onto the fingers and thumb of the glove and the bird's body and legs to the palm, over the feathers. It is a good idea to put a piece of cardboard inside the glove so the glue will not stick to the fabric on the other side. Allow the glue to dry completely.

Traditional Puppet Theater

This box has the red curtain and the bare-board stage of a traditional theater. It is made from a large, thin cardboard box and is decorated with brightly colored paper and paints. Add your own props and scenery, and you are ready for a show!

YOU WILL NEED
- Cardboard box
- Ruler
- Colored paper
- Glue stick
- Acrylic paint and paintbrush
- Pencil
- Craft knife
- Cutting mat
- Scissors
- Ribbon

1 Cover the bottom of the cardboard box with brightly colored paper. The box should be about 12 inches (30 cm) by 20 inches (50 cm). Use the glue stick to get a smooth finish and flatten out any bubbles in the paper with the palm of your hand. Then paint the sides of the box with black acrylic paint.

2 Draw curtains inside the bottom of the box — one curtain on each side. Have an adult cut along the curtain lines with a craft knife. Use a cutting mat to protect your work surface. Remove the piece of the box bottom from between the curtains.

3 Fold out one long side of the box to make the stage floor. Paint big, bold stripes on the stage floor of the theater. You can do this without a ruler, because, to get the effect of a real stage floor, the stripes should not be perfectly straight or even.

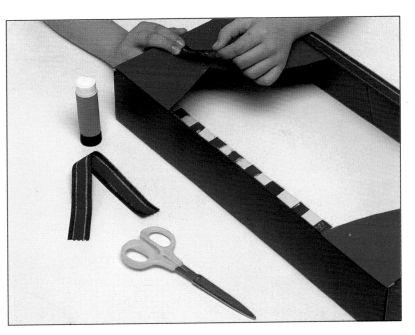

4 To finish the front of the theater, use the glue stick to attach pieces of decorative ribbon to the theater curtain.

55

Forest Theater Box

In this theater box, your puppet characters can wander through an enchanted forest. You can add a large yellow sun for a daytime scene or a shining silver moon for a nighttime setting.

YOU WILL NEED
- Cardboard box
- Scissors
- White cardboard
- Pencil
- Ruler
- Craft knife
- Cutting mat
- Colored paper
- Glue stick
- White glue and glue brush
- Fake grass
- Masking tape
- Glitter

1 Cut the lid flaps off the cardboard box with a pair of scissors. Then, place the box on a piece of white cardboard and draw around it with the pencil.

2 Draw over this pencil outline using a ruler to make the lines clear and straight. Then draw a tree-shaped border down the sides, inside the outline.

3 This border will form the front of the theater. Have an adult cut along the tree-shaped border with a craft knife. Use a cutting mat to protect your work surface.

4 Draw around the tree-shaped cardboard border on a piece of green paper. Cut out this paper outline and use the glue stick to attach it to the white cardboard. Cut a sun shape out of yellow paper and stick it to one corner of the green border with white glue.

5 Cover the outside of the box with colored paper and glue the fake grass onto the stage floor. Glue the stage border to the front of the box, holding it in place with masking tape until the glue dries. Finally, dab white glue on the trees and sprinkle them with glitter.

HANDY HINT

Ask at a local nursery for spare scraps of fake grass. If you cannot find any, you can always use green felt for the grass.

South American Bus

Finger puppets work especially well with a piece of scenery like this bus. You can attach the bus to your hand with elastic and use your other hand to work the finger puppets. Buses in South America are often decorated with brightly colored stripes, shapes, or designs.

YOU WILL NEED
- Pencil
- White cardboard
- Scissors
- Colored paper
- Two empty tape rolls
- Colored tape
- White glue and glue brush
- Glue stick
- Elastic

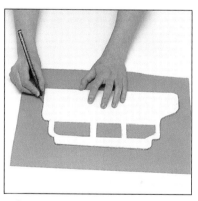

1 Draw a bus shape on white cardboard and cut it out. Carefully outline the bus shape on colored paper and cut it out.

2 For the wheels, cover two empty tape rolls with colored tape. Draw around each roll on colored paper. Cut out the two circles and stick one onto the front of each wheel with white glue.

3 Attach the colored paper bus shape to the cardboard bus with the glue stick. Cut a strip of colored paper to fit the roof of the bus and glue it on. Then use white glue to attach the wheels. Let the glue dry for at least 15 minutes. Decorate the bus with strips of colored tape.

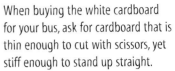

HANDY HINT
When buying the white cardboard for your bus, ask for cardboard that is thin enough to cut with scissors, yet stiff enough to stand up straight.

4 With a pair of scissors, cut four small slits in the side of the bus beneath the middle window. Thread the elastic through the slits, pulling it flat and tying it in a knot at the back. The elastic will stretch when you put your hand in it.

Sailboat

This prop is perfect for the Fishermen and Fishing Net puppet on pages 28-29. Why not make up a story with your friends that includes the Octopus and the Mermaid puppets, too?

pages 28-29

YOU WILL NEED
- Compass
- Pencil
- Stiff cardboard
- Scissors
- Colored paper
- String
- White glue and glue brush
- Wooden skewer
- Elastic

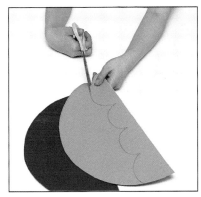

1 Use a compass and a pencil to draw a semicircle shape for the boat on a piece of stiff cardboard. Cut out this shape and use it to make two paper semicircles, one red and one blue. Draw a wavy line near the top of the blue one and another wavy line near the bottom. Cut along the two wavy lines and throw away the middle strip of blue paper.

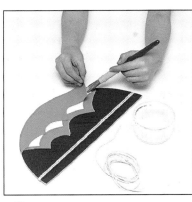

2 Glue the bottom of the blue semicircle to the bottom of the cardboard boat and the top strip of blue paper to the middle of the boat. Leave some white cardboard showing for the froth of the waves. Cut a wavy line halfway down the red semicircle and glue the top part to the top of the cardboard boat. Glue string around the top of the boat to look like a rope.

3 While the glue is drying, cut a triangular sail shape out of colored paper. Decorate the sail any way you like, then tape it onto the wooden skewer. Have an adult cut any sharp ends off the skewer.

4 Use a pair of scissors to cut four small slits in the center of the boat. Thread the elastic through the slits and tie it in back. Now you have a handy way to hold your prop.

Glossary

basis: the starting point, main part, or foundation from which something is developed or built.

boa: a long, delicate scarf, usually made of soft, wispy feathers or fluffy, lightweight fur.

clenched: pressed together tightly or closed firmly in a grip or a grasp.

dab: to press lightly or pat quickly and gently.

elegance: a superior state of richness, grace, luxury, and refinement.

expressive: effectively showing or communicating meaning or feelings.

features: the individual parts of the face, such as mouth, nose, eyes, and eyebrows.

hologram: a three-dimensional reproduction of a picture or form made by a beam of radiation, such as a laser.

host: a very large number of persons or things; an army; a multitude.

mimic: (v) to copy or imitate, often in a way that makes fun of someone or something.

plume: a large and showy bird's feather.

prop: in theater, short for "property," which is an item or object used in the performance of a play or motion picture that is not part of the scenery or a costume.

seep: to slowly leak or soak through pores or small openings.

semicircle: half of a circle.

sequins: very small, usually flat, circle-shaped pieces of glittery metal or plastic used for decoration, especially on clothing and fashion accessories.

stag: a male deer that is full grown and can usually be recognized by its antlers.

tassel: a decorative hanging ornament made from a bunch of evenly cut threads or thin cords that are knotted or tied together at the top.

template: a flat, usually stiff, piece of material with a particular shape that, when outlined, transfers that identical shape onto another piece of material or a surface.

tinsel: thin bits, strips, or strands of metal-like materials used alone for sparkly decorations or woven into fabrics or yarns to create a glittery appearance.

transform: to change the way someone or something looks or acts so much that the original person or object can no longer be recognized.

tulle: thin, delicate netting made of silk, rayon, or nylon and usually stiffened to make, for example, bridal veils and ballet costumes.

More Books To Read

Animal Crafts. Worldwide Crafts (series).
   Iain MacLeod-Brudenell (Gareth Stevens)

*Earth-friendly Toys: How to Make Toys and
   Games from Reusable Objects.* George Pfiffner
   (John Wiley & Sons)

Easy-to-Make Puppets. Mabel Duch (Plays, Inc.)

Make Your Own Performing Puppets.
   Teddy Cameron Long (Sterling)

*The Most Excellent Book of How to Be a
   Puppeteer.* Roger Lade (Copper Beech Books)

Puppet Theater Funstation. Susan Niner James
   (Price Stern Sloan)

Puppeteer Training Manual. David and
   Elaine Cole (Children's Outreach)

Puppets. World Crafts (series). Meryl Doney
   (Franklin Watts)

*Shadow Games: A Book of Hand and Puppet
   Shadows.* Bill Mayer and Peter Fox
   (Klutz Press)

*The Usborne Book of Puppets. How to
   Make* (series). Ken Haines (EDC)

Videos

Introduction to Puppet Making.
   (Bogner Entertainment)

Fun with Fabric. (Morris Video)

Make a Puppet. Kids 'n' Crafts (series).
   (Morris Video)

Making Puppets at Home. (Library
   Video Company)

Puppet Making for Children Collection.
   (Library Video Company)

Tanya the Puppeteer (MTI Film & Video)

Web Sites

www3.ns.sympatico.ca/onstage/puppets/activity/
   index.html

www.styrofoamcrafts.com/projects/fingerfr.htm

Due to the dynamic nature of the Internet, some web sites stay current longer than others. To find
additional web sites, use a reliable search engine with one or more of the following keywords: *finger
puppets, hand puppets, marionettes, puppet theaters, puppetry,* and *ventriloquism.*

Index